Presented to

_____

on _June 8, 1986_

by _First Baptist Church_

so now you're a GRADUATE

WILLIAM J. KRUTZA

BAKER BOOK HOUSE
Grand Rapids, Michigan 49506

Copyright 1981 by
Baker Book House Company

ISBN: 0-8010-5433-8

Printed in the United States of America

First printing, February 1981
Second printing, January 1982
Third printing, December 1983

CONTENTS

1. I GRADUATED...OR DID I? 7
2. IS MY DIPLOMA REALLY MINE? 11
3. THE FUTURE IS NOW 15
4. HOW IMPORTANT ARE GRADES 19
5. ALL REVVED UP AND READY TO... 23
6. YOUR FIRST GUINEA PIG AFTER GRADUATION 27
7. HANGING IT ON THE WALL 31
8. DID I EVER ANSWER THE BIG QUESTIONS? 35
9. BOOKS WERE MADE TO STAY OPEN 39
10. HABITS FOLLOW YOU LIKE HUNGRY KITTENS 43
11. NO MORE FINALS—JUST POP QUIZZES 47
12. CAN YOU BE REPLACED BY A COMPUTER 51
13. SHOULD EVERYONE WEAR BLUE JEANS? 55
14. WHEN FAILURE IS SUCCESS 59
15. SEX STILL ISN'T A REQUIRED COURSE 63
16. DID YOU LEARN TO LOVE? 67
17. DID YOU LEARN THE FOURTH "R"? 71
18. WHAT TEACHERS DID YOU LIKE? WHY? 75
19. DID YOU MEET THE WORLD'S GREATEST TEACHER? 79
20. THE SCHOOL FROM WHICH YOU'LL NEVER GRADUATE 83

I GRADUATED...
OR DID I?

1.

A GRADUATE is one who has completed a prescribed course of study.

At least that's what Webster said. And he ought to have known. He had a special way with words. He just didn't join them together like a slick politician to confuse or deceive the public. Webster said what he meant... and meant what he said.

Did he describe how you feel?

Sure did! you retort. I feel I've spent most of my life sitting in a straight-backed chair behind a school desk. Except for summer vacations, I've been brain battling books for nine months of every year ever since kindergarten days. Sometimes I thought I'd go cross-eyed reading so much. Or my head would burst... or a pile of note cards would tumble out of my ears. Wasn't there anything else to living besides school?

Hurrah! Whoopee!... and all that stuff. I've made it! I've graduated! I'm finished! Through! The end!

And I've got proof right here in black and white. The school even put a gold edge on it. Tied it with a little silky ribbon. This diploma is all mine. Mine! I think I'll hang it on the wall and invite everyone for a personal viewing. Why not? I've earned it.

Can't blame you for being excited. Even ecstatic. Most graduates feel like jumping up and down at graduation. Some leap off the stage. Others throw their mortar board hats into the audience. Some shout. A lot go out and have big parties. Graduation and celebration go together. Whoopee!

But wait a minute. That fuzzy-bearded Webster added a couple other definitions. He somehow realized that the graduate would probably feel like a releasee from an institution. Most likely he had a few releasees around the house.

Webster noticed a few other people seemed rather ecstatic about graduation day. He noticed big smiles on the faces of the releasors as well. It wasn't simply a releasee event. From the viewpoint of the graduating institution, Webster came up with this definition: "the act of graduating or promoting one into another category upon completion of a prescribed course of study. The promoting, at the close of or completion of a course of study, into a recognized standing. This recognized by the issuance of a diploma." Quite a definition! That makes it sound like the institution is as happy to graduate you as you are to be graduated. Institution employees seemed happy to see you enroll a few years ago. Now they're happy to see you leave. You've been around long enough. You've completed the necessary courses to receive their diploma. They're glad to say: Here's your diploma. Go out into the world and prove to everyone we've taught you something worth shouting about. Prove you've learned enough to make a good living. Go out and build a life upon the foundations we've helped you put in place.

Yep! You've graduated. Or if you want to get technical about it, they've graduated you!

Thank them. They've done you a favor.

They're telling the world you were good enough to meet their schooling standards. They want you to tell everyone the name of your alma mater. They want you to proudly proclaim the name. Hold it high. Shout it out. It was instrumental in helping you become the person you are . . . and the person you'll be for many months to come.

Whether you look at graduation from your point of view or from theirs, you didn't only graduate from something. You graduated into something. That something is as big as life itself. All you've learned will make your graduation into life a little smoother, exciting . . . adventurous.

Alma mater! Not a bad sounding Latin phrase. In the years ahead you'll have the opportunity to make the institution proud you were once enrolled!

IS MY DIPLOMA REALLY MINE?

2.

STUDY YOUR diploma carefully. Whose names are on it? Which name is the most important? The principal's or president's scribbled signature on the bottom line?

As far as you are concerned, if it were legal and legitimate, your diploma could have been signed by the office secretary. You could probably read the signature then!

Who cares which official signature is written at the bottom! If more than 100 diplomas were distributed on graduation day, the signature or signatures were probably printed anyway. Unless you've had some significant encounters with the person who is represented by that signature, in about five years you won't be able to describe what he looked like.

You know whose name is the most important. To you it stands out rather boldly right in the center of the diploma. You've been writing it ever since someone held your hand to help you form the letters. Most likely you wrote it before you could write all the ABCs. You can spell that name backwards in your sleep. The sound of that name is sweet music to your ears. In clear, bold print . . . or possibly in Old English to give the diploma a more sophisticated look. It's your name!

So why ask, Is my diploma mine? Of course it is! It says so in black on white. Read it for yourself.

Maybe we should look at it from a little different slant.

Look at the title page or the printed wrapper of this book. Who does it say is the author? Spell it out even if you can't pronounce it: K R U T Z A (Pronounced CREWT-ZA). Easy, wasn't it?

That's right. I wrote every word in this book . . . except for an occasional place where the editor thought he had a better idea . . . or thought he could improve my sentences. Possibly he cut out a few of my "ain'ts."

But there are a couple ways to get a book written.

Have you ever heard of ghost writers? Some books are ghost written. That doesn't mean some white-sheeted, hooded, friendly Casper took pen in hand and mysteriously produced a manuscript. What happens is this: The person whose name appears on the front of the book doesn't know how to write, yet he has a story to tell or important information to impart. He or his publisher finds someone who has journalistic skills. This journalist interviews the author and writes the book.

Come publishing time, the actual writer remains anonymous. He is a "ghost." When the publisher puts the book into print, the only name to appear on the front of the book is the one about whom it is written. Movie stars . . . television personalities . . . famous singers . . . athletes — most of them tell their stories through ghosts. The ghost writer does the actual writing, gets paid for it, but is never recognized as the true author of the book. Sometimes he is even forbidden to tell anyone he wrote the book.

A third way to write a book: The author's name (the one about whom the book is written) appears in bold print on the front. A second person's name appears directly below it in smaller print, such as "with Jack J . . .", or "as told to Jack J . . ." That says the book was a joint effort between the main author who owned most of the interesting facts but didn't know how to write them interestingly and the journalist who knew how to write interestingly but didn't have the facts until the two came together.

You ask, "What does this have to do with my diploma?"

Maybe you can figure it out.

Most graduates have to admit they didn't produce their diplomas totally by themselves. They got help . . . legitimately or not so legitimately!

Some people have to go through life admitting to their consciences that much of what brought about their diplomas was the products of ghosts. They really didn't do too much of the work. They used a variety of cribbing techniques. Or their eyeball copied from Alice, from Fred, or from whomever was sitting next to them ... especially at exam time. But the diplomas make no mention of any of these "ghosts."

Even though your diploma appears scot-free, if there are any ghosts in your educational closet, the least you could do is send them a thank you note. Maybe you'll get a few letters in return ... if you can read ghostly (invisible) ink! Such correspondence might counteract the feelings you sometimes got when you felt someone was looking over your shoulder.

If you obtained your diploma legitimately, probably you wouldn't mind if another line was added directly under yours. It could read, "In cooperation with..." An excellent way to acknowledge a few special people who injected valuable input into your life at crucial times to make your graduation possible: parents, a brother or sister, teacher or professor, some of your best friends with whom you studied, a counselor who encouraged you.

Sounds like a good idea even though it can't happen because there isn't any room on the diploma. Why not imagine it as you stare at that fancy piece of paper. Soon you'll see a name or two popping out under yours.

You'll soon discover, if you're as smart as your diploma indicates you're supposed to be, that for most of life one really can't go it alone. Anyone who gets ahead ... and is appreciated in the process ... discovers it is best to acknowledge he's succeeded "In cooperation with...."

Pity the poor fellow whose conscience continually resurrects ghosts to whom credit is due!

THE FUTURE IS NOW

3.

REMEMBER WHAT you said you wanted to be when you were in kindergarten? Doctor, nurse, fireman, airline pilot. One kindergarten straw poll indicated that nearly 75% of the little girls wanted to be nurses. The same percentage of the boys wanted to be firemen.

Thank God they grow up to consider a few of life's other 24,000 occupations! Television, parents, community affairs, school books. These all help us decide what we really want to be.

"Want to be" always points to the future. And that's what most schooling is all about. Preparation for the future.

To become a nurse takes at least 16 years of schooling. A doctor can expect 20-22 years of book learning. A commercial pilot, approximately 17 years, including Air Force flying. A trained secretary, 14 years. So if you decided on any of these professions while walking to kindergarten, you've been looking down the educational tube a long, seemingly endless time. Fortunately you really weren't able to lay out all those days end to end. They'd have reached to the. . . .

Then came graduation. Suddenly, without warning, the future is now! You've been plunked on the doorstep of your life's career.

You've found a job opening to match your educational preparation. You're happy. You sense that all the facets of your educational training have jelled together. It was worth the long struggle. If job and educational input clash, you'll wonder if you chose the wrong career. Someone might even suggest you change . . . fast!

You've placed your diploma in a dresser drawer . . . or have proudly displayed it on a wall where others notice. It indicates you are adequately trained for the task. You know your business. Suddenly there's no need to dream about the future. The future is now!

It's easy to be self-confident and cocky. Many grads are. They think book learning is all they need for success. They've been dreaming about successful blast-offs into society and the business world. Like a rocket ready to orbit the moon, Mars and Jupiter, they're all revved up.

The over-confident, like a misfired missle, readily fizzle. Startling reality becomes startling. The future dreamed about in school days is suddenly now. They might have bluffed their way through school, but on the launching pad of a career, it's performance that counts!

Everyone needs confidence, for sure. To be unafraid. But avoid being cocksure like you'd avoid chicken pox. You're entering a world of rough competition. Those who had the future dawn on them last year or a few years ago aren't about to yield to a rookie upstart. Everyone has to prove he's prepared to perform. One can't run back to his books to see how it ought to be done. Perform or fail!

Ah! There's great satisfaction when one steps into the nowness of the future for which he prepared — especially if he prepared with diligence. All the things you've studied seem to fall into the right slots. Book learning isn't just book learning. It has application. Brain-stored knowledge combined with experience, results in acceptable performance. All those demanding hours of study now prove themselves.

While the future of yesterday is now, there's still a future which is still as much future as the now was the future of yesterday. The future of expanded knowledge and know-how. The future of success. The future of new adventure.

Every time the future becomes the now . . . like right after graduation, one has to think of the future future. That keeps the now from ever becoming dull or routine.

HOW IMPORTANT ARE GRADES?

4.

AFTER HIS RETIREMENT as supreme commander of NATO forces in Europe in 1979, it was discovered that General Alexander Haig graduated lower than half-way down in his class at West Point. Yet he rose to be the top aide to one of America's presidents — actually running the entire White House staff. Next he was appointed to command all Allied military forces in Western Europe. Now he's Secretary of State.

One industrialist, who, until his death, owned the patent rights on more large earth moving machinery inventions than any other person, never graduated from high school. He quit because of discouraging grades.

You could easily add to the list. In fact, possibly you know some "dummies" who are now millionaires. Or at least they have a lot more money than you do.

And you've heard about football players, some of whom have become famous pros, who were put in all the easy college courses just to remain eligible for the football team.

Now that you're graduated, rarely will you be asked to reveal your grades. So you wonder, why were people so insistent that you get good grades? Why were they so important during school days? Why did your parents feel so defeated when you didn't get an A or a B in some course—especially in the courses in which they excelled! Why did so many students beat their brains out to get to the top of the class? Was all the effort worth it?

If you're planning to continue your education, those former grades will pop up again and again. You might have to repeat a few courses to qualify for entrance or credit at some institutions. Some schools put students on probation because of past grades. You might not get into some schools because of grades.

But what about grades and your job? The employment agency counselor probably never asked. Just what courses did you take. Where did you graduate from. Neither did the person who interviewed you in the company office.

Your boss will never ask. Clients will never ask. Even the cardiac specialist's patients never know if the doc got an A or a C in open heart surgery! Or did the company know the accountant just passed his finals or squeaked through the state certification exams.

From the viewpoint of the business world, grades don't seem important. No one seems to know why. In fact, in various parts of the country people push for the abolition of traditional grading techniques. Maybe you agree with their crusade.

But there's a more subtle meaning to your grades than what they say or whether anyone beside you or your parents are interested in knowing exactly what they were.

Of course, parents like to boast that their offspring have brains. You know all about the inheritance bit!

But grades indicate several things . . . about you!

First, a teacher or professor evaluated your grasp of the knowledge he imparted to you and fellow class attenders. He measured you against standards of performance he had worked out . . . or against the mental skills of your peers. The grades he gave to you indicated where you stood in relationship to the norms he imposed. He might have included some indication (somewhat like when you were in grammar school, when the teacher had a place on the report card which evaluated your effort in relationship to your potential) as to whether you were studying and working up to your potential.

Possibly this last point tells you the most about yourself. You know how you performed in school. You know if you worked and studied up to your potential. Of if you goofed off . . . or just got by. Were you average when you should have ranked a lot higher? Did you get Cs when you were capable of getting As or Bs? Did you strive to be the best even if others beat you to the top?

Your grades will never be posted on the company bulletin board. That would be intelligence discrimination. But those grades have been posted rather clearly in your own mind. In big, bold, black letters. You know what you got in math . . . or in English . . . or sociology.

Through the days, months and years ahead you'll still be getting grades. Others will score you high . . . or not so high. But they won't tell you. They'll just evaluate your performance . . . and reward or condemn you accordingly!

Get your report cards out and look them over. What do they tell you about your abilities, your ambition . . . and your ambitions? Now set out to prove that you can do a lot better.

If nothing else, get an A in effort!

ALL REVVED UP AND READY TO...

5.

THE MOST FAMOUS words in the auto racing world are shouted at Indianapolis each Memorial Day. "Start your engines!"

No driver needs to be told a second time. Every one is raring to go. Each has come to win the checkered flag and the big prize money.

But there's a lot of engine revving long before drivers come to the Indy 500. Engines are finely tuned. Tires are carefully checked. Maintenance crews have inspected every part of the car . . . and have repeatedly rehearsed each maintenance procedure, including how to gas up and change a tire. Every second will count in the big race. None can be lost by sloppy workmanship.

The qualifying laps on days previous to the race seem almost as important as the race itself. Each driver aims for the pole position.

Now that you've graduated, you're probably all revved up. Revved up and ready to. . . .

You've been fine tuning your brain long enough. Your mental treads can't wait to meet the road. No more need for instructors . . . or even qualifying runs. You've passed the tests. The future is yours. Full throttle ahead!

Wow! What exhuberance. How exciting. To put learned skills and amassed knowledge on the line. To plunge into making immediate contributions to the world. To produce needed products. To help alleviate needs. To change society for the better.

There's nothing stopping you now. It's green lights all along life's track. Full speed ahead.

What happens when one person is all revved up? No competition seems too stiff. No obstacles insurmountable. Move over world, I'm coming through!

Not too long after making a zooming, tire-squealing start, one realizes a few others in the race aren't quite as enthusiastic as the rookies. They're not about to let a rookie upstart outshine them. They've learned some of the tricks of the road . . . to keep upstarts in their proper place — somewhere back in the pack. To set their own pace . . . to assure themselves of coming out first at the finish line — or at least somewhere near first.

Old timers have learned one doesn't have to floor it to keep a job. They've learned they'll always have a job even if they don't operate at full throttle. They rev up . . . but only often enough and fast enough to impress the boss . . . or to keep the boss off their tails.

If at all possible, slower paced veterans aren't going to let you speed past them. They have even learned how to block an upstart's efforts . . . and make it appear it's you who is slowing up or dragging your brakes. Contrived office roadblocks. Red tape procedures. Slow downs on the assembly line. Extra toilet or coffee breaks . . . just when you need what they've been working on. Mentally punching out at least 30 minutes before quitting time. Doing a minimum amount of work, such as meeting minimum standards.

Some will even tell you to slow down. Where do you think you are going? What's the big deal? Playing up to the boss?

Others know how to flash yellow caution lights without telling you right out.

What can you do? You're all revved up and ready to pass them up. Ready to take additional responsibilities. Ready to stand in the promotion line.

An experienced Indy driver doesn't zoom past the entire field in one leap forward. He might cause too much fender scratching . . . or even planned opposition to run him off the track or into the wall!

There are better ways. He watches for his opportunity. He makes sure there's enough passing room to keep from crashing into others. Then he pushes it!

Let your superiors see, by the way you operate, that you're capable of handling an accelerated pace. Do your job thoroughly. Wait for your opportunity.

A winner keeps his mental engine well lubricated. No rusty bolts in the thinker. No loose nuts. Fine-tuned all the time. Excitingly aware of what's going on. That's one more assurance of winning.

A winner has usually learned to be tough skinned. He's able to take knocks. That's what gets top performers to the top.

Ah! There's only one checkered flag. And if you've run enough laps at the winning pace, you'll have the joy of carrying it. Otherwise, cheer the one who wins. Be a good sport.

If you're the winner, sooner or later those slower-paced people will have to admit you have what it takes to be out front. Who knows . . . they might even begin revving up a little bit more themselves. They don't want to be left in your dust!

YOUR FIRST GUINEA PIG AFTER GRADUATION

6.

GUINEA PIGS. Mice. White rats. Rabbits. Experimental animals in scientific laboratories. Innocent creatures subjected to all types of experimentation. Injected with all types of chemicals to see what will kill them . . . or make them live better! Often used to determine the values and safety of humanly ingested chemicals, foodstuffs.

Scientific experiments. For better health. For safety. For more enjoyment. To produce better products.

But the poor guinea pigs don't think so. They're victims . . . not victors. Nobody ever asks them if they want a big overdose! Like the daily injections of saccharin which equaled those consumed by a 135 pound human drinking 80 bottles of pop per day for 25 years! Punch drunk pigs!

We've developed a phrase from all this laboratory experimentation. When we want to test something, such as a kitchen-concocted recipe, we ask someone, "Will you be my guinea pig?"

Sometimes they agree. Sometimes not.

Sometimes we don't tell them it's our latest gourmet experiment. They're guinea pigs just the same!

If they like the concoction, we boast that we originated it. If they don't like it, we admit we hadn't tried that recipe before. Better luck next time!

But many people are guinea pigs at far more serious levels. What about the first patients in a dentist's office? Or of a new doctor in a hospital operating room? Or those subjected to the latest radioactive experimenters?

Not much leeway for error then! Can't say it was a big experiment. If it works, great. If it doesn't — oops! The scalpel slipped! The drill went too deep! The radiation penetrated too far!

These would be serious cases. Worthy of malpractice suits.

But what about the less serious experimentation? We all have to practice our learned skills . . . or the ones we didn't learn too well. On someone . . . sometime . . . somewhere!

Maybe it's your first office job. Your first sales approach. The first time you pushed the button to rev up a large engine.

Scared? You try not to show it. But don't apologize. Such initial fear is good. It helps prevent cockiness. Helps you keep your head screwed down. Your feet on the floor.

You can't tell everyone around you you're a rookie... or that they are guinea pigs. That you are trying out your book learning for the first time. They'd never let you get started.

Who'd want to risk the surgeon's first incision? Or even the barber's first haircut?

All you can do is treat human guinea pigs with special care. Be thoroughly prepared to do your work. Don't inject things you know little or nothing about. Don't start by trying to impress others with your knowledge. That'll backfire. They'll detect you don't really know as much as you make off you know. They'll become suspicious... and even unsympathetic. Don't be afraid to let the guinea pigs squirm a little when you come at them.

Keep your ears and eyes open. Learn procedures. Then follow them closely until you've become experienced. People around you catch on real fast when they sense you're bluffing... of if they know you're cutting your working teeth at their expense.

Sure, we all need guinea pigs. Everyone has to start sometime... somewhere. We've all needed those upon whom we've experimented... or we've been that particular laboratory species ourselves! Only experience can help anyone graduate from the experimental laboratory into the world of experience. Hopefully, in the process, not too many guinea pigs will be overdosed by the unintentional mistakes we make along the way.

Thank God, antidotes are available. Others catch on fast... and sometimes human guinea pigs turn around and show the greenhorn experimenter how to do the task. Be thankful they are around.

One should never say "Those dumb guinea pigs!" If possible, some of them should say, "That dumb experimenter."

So if you make a guinea pig squeal, try to smooth his fur! He'll probably become friendly in the process.

HANGING IT ON THE WALL
7.

HAVE YOU EVER wondered, when you've walked into your doctor's or dentist's office, why they have their college degrees hanging on the wall? Or why your minister displays his? Or the local pharmacist?

Required by law in some states . . . at least for the medicine mixers. But most likely not for the preacher!

Kind of nice to know your dentist got the proper drilling credentials. Or the doc graduated from a recognized scalpel school. You feel a little safer knowing they've been properly trained.

There they are. Under glass. In unpretentious black picture frames.

Maybe it's just pride that motivates these degree displayers and displays... or special certifications... or ministerial ordinations. They've got a right to be proud. Degrees, diplomas, certifications... all quietly proclaim what institutions have proclaimed them worthy to practice on you. It's right out in the open... usually in not-too-easy-to-read Old English!

You graduated. That diploma or degree is all yours. Whether you majored in medicine or mechanics. Whether in pharmacy, podiatry or plumbing. Or in truck driving.

It might look a little ridiculous if everyone who graduated from high school, technical school, private college, university, or from some specialized courses, suddenly put his diploma in a black frame, knocked a nail into a nearby wall, and displayed the fact he was a trained worker.

Most likely a lot of employers wouldn't allow it. They'd call it all nonsense. Some might mutter that it isn't the diploma that counts. Just perform!

So you can't hang yours on the office or factory wall! Don't feel miffed. It has special meaning to you. Don't forget that! Find a niche at home. Like the bedroom wall ... or in the den... or in the hallway. Alongside other certificates of significance in your family: baptism certificates... the wedding license... special job or company recognitions... sports awards... state certifications.

There's nothing wrong in quietly telling the world you've had recognized knowledge injections. You've studied. You've performed at better-than-normal capacities. You've accomplished something out of the ordinary. You've met or surpassed the set standards of your area of interest.

That's what diplomas are all about. Recognition.

So what's wrong with having yours out where not only others can see them, but where you can see them. To remind you of your skills and knowledge. To prod you on to use those skills and knowledge.

A gallery of diplomas. Not a bad idea.

But if you don't have such a niche, at least put all your paper awards into one of those photo albums with the see-through plastic pages.

And look through those see-through pages occasionally! Like on the anniversary date of your graduation... or when you need an extra shot of enthusiasm about your skills. Those "look at what I have earned" sessions will be as satisfying as the doctor or dentist passing the one's they display on their office walls! That's your name there!

DID I EVER ANSWER THE BIG QUESTIONS?

8.

QUESTIONS! Every student's cranium has been bombarded with more than its share. At the end of almost every chapter of every school book. Asked by most teachers... especially at pop quiz and final exam times.

Whew! Glad graduation has come. No more questions... unless you could turn the tables on the educational process and ask a few yourself.

What's the big idea asking whether I ever answered the *big* questions? Big ones! How do you think I earned my diploma? Do you think I majored in trivia? Some of my teachers possessed special skills in question production—both in quantity and quality. And they almost always expected big answers—the brain teasing kind.

I'm sure you'd put a lot of the interrogations one answers in high school college or graduate school into the "big questions" department. What big questions are still unanswered?

Not complex, four or five syllable worded questions. Not ones you'll need an open book to answer. These big questions search for meanings that must come from your inner resources. From what you are as a person.

Try these on for size:
> What is the basic meaning of life?
> Why are we here?
> What are life's most important goals?

Pretty big questions! What kinds of answers have you come up with in the past? Did your education produce satisfactory replies? Did you ever seriously face such questions?

All the way through school, you've heard you were the result of some apes monkeying around a few million years ago. Somehow that answer seemed as plausible as the moon being made of phosphorescent Wisconsin Swiss cheese! You have to overstretch your imagination every time you look into a mirror. You don't believe what you see there originated in apeland.

If you're just some quadruped which suddenly stood upright or got his tail detatched when he pinched his tail in the crotch of a tree, why not head back to the jungle? You'd avoid all the tensions and frustrations of human existence.

Now that you've graduated, it's time to cast aside such unscientific theories about the origins of man and really seek and explore some satisfactory answers.

Jews, Protestants, Catholics . . . and even Islamic believers . . . know they're not overgrown or smoothly shaven apes. Take a good look at the first couple of chapters of the Bible. Any version. Digest its concepts. The first three words of the Bible make a lot more sense than a book full of unproven evolutionary hypotheses.

You have a lot more than instincts and sexual cravings, you have power to reason. Superior communicative abilities. A complex personality. And when you scientifically examine your own personality, it's appreciatively easier to accept the concept of being created in the image of God — the ultimate personality — than to believe ancient ancestors fell upward out of tropical trees. Saturate yourself with the concepts of the early chapters of the Bible and you'll soon be able to walk uprightly proud . . . like you ought!

Besides, you'll begin to discover some of the basic meanings of life. Especially if you couple your Genesis reading with that of the biblical Proverbs, Psalms, and the New Testament. See what Jesus Christ had to say about life!

You won't suddenly turn into a religious freak. Not if you study the Bible with the same open mind you were supposed to use in studying science. It makes more sense than a lot of biology or psychology. And about a third of the way through the New Testament, in the first chapter of John, you'll come across this tremendous statement: "In Him was life, and that life was the light of men."

Try that on for meaning in life!

After making that a part of your inner being, you can go to why are we here and what are life's most important goals.

To exist? To have sex?

If those are one's main goals, one still has a pygmy personality. He's to be pitied . . . not proud!

Digest a little more of the world's greatest book and come up with the most satisfying and meaningful answers.

Big questions require you to go to the sourcebook which has the biggest answers. And you know that the biology book isn't even the most important book you studied in school! Nor is your math or English book. Which other book would you put in this category. Take it from the masters of the past . . . those who have readily and really studied the best of books. Like Abe Lincoln who stated that no one is educated until he has read and studied the Bible. It's the book with the biggest answers.

How many of the big questions have you answered so far?

BOOKS WERE MADE TO STAY OPEN

9.

BOOKS! Don't talk to me about books. I just graduated. My books are where they belong — on the bookshelf. I'm going to leave them there for a while.

Some students, especially college students, keep all their books. A big investment. References for the future.

Others can't wait until quarters or semesters end to cart their texts down to the used book counter. Cash on the line is better than books on the shelf.

Still others take a selective approach. Keep the most important books . . . or ones which will be needed to refresh one's memory . . . or to learn what was missed during school days . . . or the ones which simply look good on the shelf, adding to the decor of the room.

One can sympathize with the post-graduation closed-book syndrome. Give the eyes ... and the brain ... some needed relaxation.

Give me a little time to put book learning into practice. Time to show classroom facts actually penetrated my thick skull. Time to show that book learning has applicationability.

Anyway, haven't we already talked about joining the working world? That's what I'm doing right now.

But the fellow who makes the most impact on the working world is the one who keeps his brain door open. None of his books have zippers!

A diploma doesn't mean the graduate has learned all the facts in all his books . . . or has 100% recall. Some learned a minimum. There's only one class valedictorian!

When it comes to job time, you might need to keep a few books open. Even have them at your fingertips on your desk or workbench.

Unfortunately, far too many graduates take the closed book approach to life. You know them — people who graduated several years ago. Read nothing beyond the newspaper and the TV guide. They think they know it all. Nothing more to learn ... except from the school of hard knocks.

You'll soon discover which people have carefully maintained the closed book approach to living ... who almost seem to relish the closed book syndrome.

You've just begun to learn. In any career, even in a lifetime of learning, no one can ever know it all. Learning is a continuous process. And it adds adventure to life. Makes life much more interesting. Can't get bored when you study something new. New ideas are like fresh water... always welcome when life seems a little dry.

Who knows it all, anyway? In most areas of life, such as in the career you have chosen, an individual has a difficult time learning only a small segment of what can be known. We must become specialists in one area... like computer programming... or metallurgy... or mathematics....

Got to keep the books open... and purchase the latest editions... attend special seminars... get the best magazines.

Someplace along the line one of your teachers probably said books are man's best friend. Took the place of the old adage about a dog being so friendly. Really the teacher had open books in mind. Not shelf decor. The ones you study regularly.

Keeping the brain door open. It's your choice!

HABITS FOLLOW YOU LIKE HUNGRY KITTENS

10.

MEOW! Meow! There's something touching about a little kitten's cry. Irresistible. But once you give in, you're hooked.

Hungry kittens learn fast. Follow the leader... especially the person with food. Meow for more. Soon become pesty. Soon you can't shake them. No matter where you go, the little fur balls follow. Like Mary's little lamb which got mixed up in a school classroom.

An 11-year-old named her kitten Habit. Short for Bad Habit, she said. Followed her everywhere... even into the bathroom. Drank out of the potty. Cried in the middle of the night. Repeated these nasty practices continually.

When someone would say "nice kitty" to the calico feline, the little girl had other thoughts, "You should only know!"

It ain't only kittens that follow us around. Habits are much like hungry kittens. They are always tagging along right at our heels.

Everyone develops habits. Good ones and bad ones. No matter where one turns, there's a habit letting its presence be known. Meow!

Kittens keep coming back as long as you feed them. Love a little meower and you'll love it for life . . . or it'll love you for life. You like the way it brushes up against your legs. Rolls over right in front of you. Jumps into your lap. Purrs like a steady running engine. We even say of engines, big or small, "It purrs like a kitten."

Who wouldn't want to treat some of his habits like he'd treat hungry kittens. Feed them. Let them become full grown. Groom them to make them more attractive. Fine tune them until they operate as smoothly and appreciatively as a purring kitty.

Some of these kittenlike habits include: social graces such as opening doors for others, letting others take the largest portion of food, yielding the right-of-way on the highway or at a city intersection, good eating manners, giving kind replies when others fly off the handle, good grooming — including the use of deodorants . . . and many more.

Feed such habits a rich diet of sociological and psychological vitamins. Make the diet complete. Add a few extra minerals every so often. Sharpen new social graces. Remember the admonition, "Be kind to one another. . ." That takes in a lot of developed habits you want to be known by.

But let's face it. Sometimes kittens become obnoxious cats. They grow furniture-scratching nails. They bite and fight.

Scat, cat! That's how one soon feels. If only he could get rid of Habit. Especially Bad Habit.

Bad habits like ornery kittens: get out of my way, I'm coming through, me first, what I do is my own business, sloppy dress, poor grammar or speech, personal pleasure first — that's all that counts, do as little work as possible, unnecessary use of necessary drugs, the nicotine habit.

The list of ornery kittens seems to be unending. It seems that Bad Habit is prodigiously reproductive. Breeding all the time. And coming up with some amazing mixtures. One Bad Habit might resemble another, but there are some distinct markings . . . especially when they are bred with somone else's Bad Habit.

How does one rid himself of an unwanted kitten?

Take it to the animal shelter. They have ways with cats!

Quit feeding it so it goes away.

Donate it to a neighbor.

We've developed some ingenious ways of getting rid of unwanted kittens. But no one really wants our Bad Habits!

Maybe the best way to get rid of a bad habit is one we'd never want to practice on kittens: starve it to death. Whenever one of your bad habits meows for attention, decide not to feed it. We feed our habits when we practice them. And if we refuse the bad habit any food, it soon disappears. Like throwing away the cigarettes we still have in the pack and absolutely refusing to spend any money for more.

Sure you'll miss the meowing of a Habit for awhile. But try feeding the good habits. They purr... and that's a lot more satisfying sound than the meowing!

Once your bad habit has left home, you'll discover that the good ones have a lot more to offer. Like good evening companionship. And when others come into your presence and hear the purring, they'll take notice. Some will even comment on how much they enjoy the activity.

Love those good little kittens!

NO MORE FINALS — JUST POP QUIZZES

11.

NO MORE FINALS. Sounds like a student's paradise. Where is this new school? Who are the teachers? Why wasn't I enrolled a long time ago?

Call it the school of life. Right where you are. Doing what you are doing. At work. During social contacts. At home. While traveling. Everywhere.

Nobody's going to give you final exams. Those are all behind you now. Remember, you graduated.

Just before graduation you probably stayed up late many nights . . . cramming your cranium. Even prayed you'd remember the important facts. Did a lot of memorizing. Experimented with some actual problems.

Went over your notes once again. Prayed some more. Maybe you squeaked by. Just passed the exam. Or maybe you lucked out and got the top grade in the class. Maybe you heard a teacher say, "Well done!"

You've written your last final—at least for a while. You're not heading back into the classroom tomorrow.

But don't rejoice too quickly. You've entered a new era. It's the era of continual pop quizzes. Someone will come up with some dillies wanting immediate answers.

Remember those pop quizzes teachers pulled on you. You'd come to class expecting a lecture, discussion or experiment. Possibly you thought of sleeping during the class hour.

Surprise, surprise! The teacher pulled out a short quiz. Maybe it lasted 15 minutes... or the entire period.

Sometimes you were thoroughly prepared. Sometimes not. Sometimes you tried to bluff your way through. Fortunately the teacher had a formula in which pop quizzes equaled less than half of your final grade... most often only one-third.

In the school of life, there's no place for finals. That would mean termination . . . entrance to eternity. If some employer wants to give you a final, it means your job is terminated. Not a quiz. He doesn't want more information from you. He's saying goodbye!

Life just keeps going. So pop quizzes keep coming.

Someone is always around to ask questions . . . and expect answers. Sometimes when you least expect it. Sometimes with questions you've never faced before. Sometimes to challenge your position. Sometimes to determine if you are as capable as your diploma suggests. Sometimes just because they don't know how to answer the question and are genuinely seeking your help.

Some pop questions are short . . . easy to answer. Sometimes they are complex brain busters. Sometimes you'll think the questioner took an advanced course in question making.

And the most humiliating aspect of it all is when you have to answer, "I don't know."

But that might be the best answer! Then you have to go do some homework. Open those books again!

How do you prepare for pop quizzes? How did you prepare during good old school days? By keeping up to date in your studying. By constantly reviewing the teacher's notes. By doing your homework. By doing collateral reading assignments.

Answering life's pop quizzes demands the same requirements. Being ready all the time. Up to date. Answering in a manner to satisfy the questioner. Knowing your subject.

Pop quizzes keep one on his toes. Keep the cobwebs from forming on the crossbeams of the brain. Challenge one to keep the brain cells active.

But they also do something in life situations that they don't do in the classroom. They help others in their search for knowledge . . . for answers to the why of living. Possibly even help others get promotions.

Life's pop quizzes can also govern whether you get promoted. Superiors want to know if you know enough to advance. They'll pop the questions when you least expect it.

So no matter who the questioners may be, there's no alternative to that good old Boy Scout motto, "Be prepared!"

Prepared to give acceptable answers. Prepared to perform to meet the demands placed upon your abilities. Prepared to work at maximum capacity. Prepared to react to challenges to your brain storage tank.

Fret not. No matter where you turn, someone's going to test your brain power. They're going to demand an answer — now . . . not later! Not on some final exam.

Every day is pop quiz time. Expect it. And when you have opportunity, pop a few pop quizzes of your own.

There are no more finals...until...! And then you'd better be prepared. The final quizmaster is the One who created the brain in the first place. And His questions deal with the meanings you've found in life. His questions will deal with the *big questions* . . . and the big answers you've discovered . . . or if you only know small answers!

CAN YOU BE REPLACED BY A COMPUTER?

12.

THE COMPUTERIZED society. It's here. You're a part of it. Victim or victor — take your pick!

Wherever you turn, a computer has been there before you. In the grocery store . . . hardware store . . . doctor's office . . . school classroom . . . business office . . . farm. You name it. We've computerized it.

Just feed a program card into a computer and a doctor can discover whether you've had your tonsils removed, your blood pressure regulated . . . or if you've been periodically bothered by diarrhea.

Such medical info is extremely valuable. The doc can more readily determine your present ailments . . . and prescribe a quick-acting cure. Possibly at less expense! Or just the push of a computer button will tell some school admissions director whether the school sees any potential in you as a graduate student. Instant transcripts of courses . . . and grades! Sorry, Charlie!

Computerized bills. We all get them. All your credit accounts are on computer. Your bank statements came out of an electronic accounting machine. Figures the exact amount of interest you owe on a loan . . . or what the bank is willing to pay on your savings.

Ever argue with a computer? Almost a losing battle. You continue to get the computer's readout. Says you owe the company a certain amount. Keeps sending you the bill.

One time I owed a major oil company $83.56 for gasoline. My monthly computerized bill showed this amount . . . plus interest. Something had gone wrong within the computer's electronic brain. The monthly interest charge was listed as $34,319.10. Wow!

I wrote a letter to "Dear Oil Company Computer: You have slipped your electronic gears!"

It took a couple months to correct. And you guessed it. I received a computer typed letter stating the company was sorry for the computer's error.

Victim!

On another occasion my local bank sent the monthly statement. The computer showed I had $200.00 more in my account than I had figured. I inquired about this, but because I had thrown away my latest statement, the bank accounting department said nothing could be done. The computer only kept figures in its mechanized head for just two months. I had gained $200.00. Victor!

Some people worry about computers. There's too much information stored in their miniaturized circuits. Too much that should be kept secret that is available to too many researchers.

Invasion of privacy will be a constant problem. And an ever increasing problem as computers become more sophisticated and more segments of our society resort to using these electronic memory machines.

In fact, some believe sooner or later most people could be replaced by computers. Just pick their brains for a few new ideas, punch these onto computer cards, feed them into the memory bank and then draw them out whenever needed.

Everyone, especially the new graduate, has to ask himself if he's a prime candidate for being replaced by a computer. Will some electronic brain take the place of genuine human gray matter?

It's possible . . . if. . .

☐ If you don't continue to think for yourself. If you get lazy headed and don't come up with new and refreshing thoughts. If you simply accept what others say about life. If you let some punched out cards represent what you believe about important subjects. If you've joined the closed book brigade.

Let others do your thinking for you and sooner or later you'll suddenly wake up to discover an electronic machine has been placed where you formerly sat in office or factory or store.

But have no fear of ever being replaced by a computer

☐ If you think for yourself. Never joining the "me too" crowd even if it's the parade of your peers. Coming up with your own ideas on how you're going to live, what direction your future is going to take, whom you'll submit to, what you'll do with your leisure time.
☐ If you come up with some creative ideas. Invent something. Put old concepts together in new, exciting, adventurous ways. Make your home atmosphere one-of-a-kind in style and decor.
☐ If you develop those characteristics which make for leadership, not followership. Leaders always are out front. They can't be computerized. They might use computers . . . but always discover new and untried processes by which to use electronic information.

Replaced by a computer? It's really up to each person. Either allow yourself to be reduced to a lot of holes on a computer input card or else be the one who holds the cards!

Actually, the graduate faces some options: be computerized . . . or be the computerizer.

SHOULD EVERYONE WEAR BLUE JEANS?

13.

EXCEPT for the drab dress of the 800 million mainland Chinese, blue jeans are the next most popular form of dress around the world. And even the Chinese are catching on!

Blue jeans started out as a USA exclusive. But that didn't last long. Soon you found tight fitting-denims in Bangkok... and Budapest... and Brussels.

Billings... Birmingham... Batavia... Brownsville... Boston. Blue jeans dominate the bottom half. Male and female created we them.

It's been a coon's age since we could point someone out by saying "She's the one wearing jeans!"

How many pairs do you have? Ever wear anything else?

Favorite brand or no label, they're still jeans. Blue is standard. But the other colors are making appearances.

Since jeans have been such a favorite form of dress, we've begun to look at them as the most convenient and easiest to maintain clothing to wear. Wash and wear... possibly without even being touched by an electric iron.

But there's still a subtle, if not compelling, conformity about blue jean wearing.

A freshman college student declared to his mother, "Everybody wears jeans. That's all they wear on campus. Why do you want me to be an odd ball?"

Jean-wearing often indicates our submission to peer group pressure. Consciously or subconsciously. Wouldn't dare to be different. Why stand out? Who wants to be the odd one?

But such an attitude might also indicate our willingness to be followers, not leaders. To be conformists, not trend setters. To be a part of the crowd, not individualists.

Society seems to have particular powers to squeeze all of us into standard molds. Advertising urges us all to use accepted standardized brands. Crowd psychology gets us to all laugh at the same jokes or move to the same beat. How easily we're excited to shout in unison at football or basketball games.

Conformists. That's what we so easily become. Doing it like everyone else. Joining the crowd. Lining up with the peer group.

Blue jeans can be just one symptom of that conformity.

Of course, it isn't always true. Some rugged individualists wear jeans!

Should everyone wear them?

Not if you want to be individualistic. Not if you want to express a new leadership.

Whether in jeans or red slacks, the need in our society is for people who proclaim their individuality. Those who dare to stand out and be different from the crowd.

Individuals energetically thinking beyond conformity. Who devise better ideas. New ideas. Who search out new manners of expression. Who keep inventive genius alive.

Leaders in almost every aspect of society have been non-conformists. Once you've joined the conformist crowd you've become a follower. Not a leader. Another must step forward into the leadership position.

Of course, you can't be a leader all the time. Those who claim such position become ego maniacs. Often dangerously dictatorial. We don't need any more such people. The world already has its share.

It's okay to be a follower sometime. But even then one needs to keep his eyes wide open to maintain an individuality which expresses creativity and maturity.

And there's an even greater need in the world for such creative leadership in the moral realm. To set new standards about sex . . . to get it out of the rut of momentary body pleasure and bring it into its richest meanings.

Or honesty. Or a new sense of the worth of work. Or integrity. Or practicing the golden rule.

All places for leadership. Inviting you to step out from the conforming crowd and really express mature individuality. All looking for non-conformists to lead into new vistas of a better society.

If your blue jeans have the same label as everyone else's . . . if you're a strict conformist, isn't it time you had another graduation — into the realm of individualism?

WHEN FAILURE IS SUCCESS

14.

BECOME a millionaire in five years. Develop a winning personality in nineteen easy-to-follow lessons. Have hundreds of friends.

Promises. Promises. Promises. All on how to become successful . . . fast!

We're wired for success. Everything in life has to be better or bigger than the past. More is the measure of the prosperous person.

That's why you graduated. All those years of schooling for one main purpose: the successful life.

Money . . . position . . . poise . . . pleasure.

And the seemingly highest success — to be able to do

what you want when you want as fully as you want.

Most of us can't wait to become rich. Why does it take so long? Can't we come up with a scheme? What about the one advertised in the latest magazine we bought? How about joining Entrepreneur, Inc.?

And it all looks so simple. Make $100 a week — parttime. On weekends! Collect outstanding royalties or commissions after your first six months. Sounds too good to be true. So we send a check or money order for the $12.95 asking price.

Sometimes the scheme works . . . especially for the person collecting our $12.95!

Become a successful person. Learn how to get people to work for you . . . and enjoy it! The old Dale Carnegie course rewritten: How to Win Friends and Influence People.

Add personality power to your money making bonanza. That's the ultimate of success!

Or is it?

What do we mean about failure being success? Isn't that contradictory?

Sometimes the greatest personality developers are not those which place us on easy street, but those which lead us down a rocky road. Tin cups instead of silver platters. Rebuffs rather than quick acceptances.

Failures often lead to successes. Especially in the development of our inner selves.

Here are a few failures that spell success.

Failure to give in to those who think sex is a game.

That makes for a successful evaluation of our own sexuality. We discover ourselves as mature personalities, not simply bodily toys with which others play.

Failure to yield to the temptation to use drugs for entertainment purposes.

This keeps one's head clear at all times. Clear to think logically. To think imaginatively. To be in full control of ourselves in every situation.

Sure there are drug highs. Alcohol highs. Marijuanna highs.

But none of these are as great as the high of a creative mind . . . and the wonderfully successful and exciting products such a mind can formulate.

Failure to cheat or lie.

Providing things honest in the sight of all men. Never having to learn false facts so we can repeat the truth without a slip-up. Even when truth might cost us more. Or demand more of our time. Of winning the scoffing of cheaters.

The non-cheater never has to invent a story. He never has to remember a lie. Truth is his best defense. He can tell it anytime, anyplace, to anybody.

But one can also succeed by failing in those things he was expected to succeed in. Like going bankrupt in a business deal. How often one learns more about business through bankruptcy than through booms. Or his personality matures because he's forced to travel the rough road.

Choose failure wisely. And don't apologize when you fail. Especially at anything which is morally wrong. Carry your chin high. The most dynamic successes are those who've done the same. Join the crowd who can rightfully be proud they've succeeded at failing at the appropriate times in the appropriate things.

SEX STILL ISN'T A REQUIRED COURSE

15.

SEX EDUCATION. Everyone needs it. And blessed is the person who got it straight. Who knows the true facts... and knows the seriousness of knowing the facts.

Production and pleasure. That's what sex is all about. Producing new life. Enjoyment.

So get the facts straight.

The possibility of producing a human life is both wonderful and awesome. All possible in one sexual encounter. A human . . . just like yourself. Inheriting some of your good traits... and some of your not-so-good ones! A human with potentials for growth, creativity, leadership...or just being a tag-along follower. A very healthy specimen of humanity...or a weak sickling. Possible from one quick sperm shot!

But sex isn't limited to human reproduction. In fact, most people approach it entirely from the point of personal pleasure. It's enjoyable! That's why "everyone's doing it!"

At least that's what most people think.

Let's backtrack a little. When you had classroom sex education, that gave you the facts. It was academic... not experimental. It wasn't a laboratory course. Nobody ever demanded that you'd pass the course after bedroom performance. Or you'd get a better grade after experimenting. The teacher presented the facts... male and female.

Hopefully you took the academic approach. Got the facts straight. Didn't engage in private laboratory testing as you gained a new idea.

If you've gone through more than 12 years of schooling and can still claim virginity, be proud. There's a lot to say for self-control . . . and reserving the tingling of your desires for your marriage partner.

Now that you're graduated, you'll discover a goodly number of people who think you probably got at least B+ in sex education... and want to enter the laboratory stage. They're not interested in teaching you more . . . except "tricks!" They've got one main idea in mind —pleasure. Their own! Yours is probably secondary, especially if you're a female.

Maybe these graduated sex experimenters will laugh at your desire for virginity or abstinence (if you've experimented during schooling days.) Let them. It's your choice. Your body. And there's something to be said for someone who practices what the old timers called self-control.

Sometimes sex goes with the job . . . or that's one of the demands. Not on the application form. But after you've been around a short while. Secretaries are often expected to be sex partners. Or to be the "something extra" when any business associates arrive from out of town.

The original creator of human sex had in mind a combination of production and pleasure. The pleasure to bind the producers together. To keep them attracted to one another. And even though we've got all types of fool-proof birth control methods and devices . . . or could indulge in abortions, that wasn't the original intention. Sex and marriage go together.

Prudish. Maybe. But if it isn't too late for you to discover the values of this approach, you'll be glad you reserved your sex orgasms and organs to bind you to a permanent lover who enjoys the same last name as your own.

Don't be kidded into believing that sex is a required course in which everyone freely indulges . . . and ends up with a special certificate. Just ask a few people who've given in to the laboratory approach and you'll discover that experimentation isn't all it's cracked up to be.

Interview a few who've reserved sex as a cementing force to keep their marriage exciting and enjoyable. You'll discover they've found a better way. Sex means a lot more than a tingly feeling. It's a lot more than an exciting, impetuous bedroom game with a sudden conclusion.

If someone insists that sex is required to keep a job... or to keep a friendship... don't be afraid to challenge them to define why. Demand that they respect your body... and your principles. That's a good way to bring sex into its proper perspective... and help others discover one of the strengths of your personality... and some of the other good things about you which were developed in classes other than the ones which dealt with human reproduction.

According to the Good Book, there's only one place in which sex is required. Adam and Eve were the first to discover this!

DID YOU LEARN TO LOVE?
16.

SEX AND LOVE. Aren't they synonymous?

You can have sex without love. Probably you know some good examples. People who've engaged in anonymous sexual encounters... some on a first name basis only. Swingers who only swing once. Those who bedded down on a dare... or to be accepted by peers. Those who felt raped... or who were literally raped. Those who engaged while drunk or high, not knowing what happened until it was all over... or the next morning... or when they discovered that they were in need of a pregnancy test.

When sex is mainly done for physical or emotional

reasons, love (genuine love) can easily be an absent ingredient.

Of course you can have love without sex!

The love of a mother or father for a child. The love of one friend for another — regardless of being male or female. The love one has toward those who really never love in return . . . or who can't love. Like mistreated children, or some handicapped, or emotionally disturbed.

Maybe what we need more than anything else is a good definition of love.

We know what is meant by sex. Sexual relations. Affairs. Orgasms.

But what is love?

Back in B.C. some southern Europeans spent a lot of time discussing the meaning of love. They weren't satisfied with the concept of bodily expression only. They came up with three basic meanings for love. As the saying goes, the Greeks had a word for it. In this case, three words. Talked about the three levels of love.

Yeah! They believed in sex. Had plenty of time not only to think about it, but practice as well.

Love level #1: *Eros.* Sensual love. That excitingly warm emotional feeling that draws a member of one sex to a member of the opposite sex. Hand holding. Hugging. Kissing. Sexual encounter. All the way.

No one is quite sure what chemical combinations . . . or emotional electrical charges, excite eros. In some cases a male might come in close contact with a female for several years without any eros excitation. Then suddenly it hits. Like lightning. No one knows why. Maybe you've had such an experience.

Love level #2: *Phileo*. Friendship love. That bond of commitment which binds friends together. The willingness to help a friend in need. To be available to help. The joy of giving others a part of your life. The joy of being together with someone on your special people list.

We all love friends . . . or at least one friend. That special person who seems to understand us better than others . . . and one whom we understand likewise. A person to whom we'll readily expose our inner self. One with whom we'll share our troubles . . . one with whom we can't wait to share our joys.

We've built up this special relationship. We love this special person. And there isn't any eros involved!

Eros is as far from our minds as dawn is from sunset. Pure, enjoyable, meaningful friendship love.

Love level #3: *Agape*. The Greeks called this God love. Love on the highest level. And the best source of examples is the Bible. Here are a couple: "For God so loved the world that he gave his one and only son, that whoever believes in him shall not perish but have eternal life" (John 3:16); "But God demonstrated his own love for us in this: While we were still sinners, Christ died for us" (Romans 5:8).

In relationship to our treatment of others, Jesus gave this simple commandment: "Love one another." Demonstrate the same type of love toward others that God has demonstrated toward us.

What is agape love? Self-giving love. Love that considers the other person before it considers itself. Love that gives without expecting something in return. Love that goes out of its way to be helpful. Sacrificial love.

Agape in contrast to eros: self-giving rather than self-gratifying. In contrast to phileo: expecting nothing in return rather than knowing the loved will reciprocate.

Learning the meanings of love is the first step to learning to love. One has to get beyond the academics. Into the laboratory of life. In fact, get beyond experimentation. Especially with agape. Practice it.

Which state of love dominates your life? Eros — emotional involvement and enjoyment. Phileo — mutual sharing and friendship. Agape — sacrificial giving of yourself on behalf of those in need.

As one looks out upon needy humanity, if he only practices the first two levels of love, he'll soon be known as a greedy, self-serving person. And we have plenty of such people around us.

It takes a kind of graduation to go from level to level. But you're capable. You've graduated before.

Why stay in the standing line for Level #1 when so many graduate courses are available in the other two levels? Level #3 always seems to have the most vacancies. Graduate up higher!

DID YOU LEARN THE FOURTH "R"?

17.

READING. 'Riting. 'Rithmetic. Three essentials for graduation. Especially from high school. No one ever tests your penmanship when you enter... or are ready to leave, college. It's too late by then.

Did you learn how to read? Special classes in speed reading. Comprehension drills. Learning how to skim.

And that third R — short for arithmetic. Knowing that $1+1=2$ or that $x+y=z$. Or fractions. Adding. Subtracting. Multiplying. Dividing. Those four basic forms of math in using the world of numbers.

The three "R"s. Essential to getting a job. Essential to getting along in life. Such as reading road signs or maps.

Adding up the grocery bills. Subtracting on your checkbook stubs. Writing your name on the bottom line of a check. Reading an instruction manual when you have to assemble some newly purchased home product.

These three "R"s are as essential to life as food. No one has to come up with better, easier-to-learn, substitutes. You'd even have to know how to read to learn the substitutes. Even new math is math. And reading is still reading.

Some grads swear they'll never read another book as long as they live. They've become word weary. But you'll read the rest of your life. Even if it's only the words of TV commercials. Cereal box tops. Soap wrapper words. Or the scores of your favorite sport teams.

So you might as well put a few books on your eye exercise list.

And keep your pencils sharp for those other two "r"s. They'll come in handy too.

So what's this about a fourth "R"? Didn't the schools teach us enough already? Could they teach this fourth "R"?

Religion.

"Religion!" you exclaim. "No wonder I didn't get it in school. It's unconstitutional to teach one specific religion in the public school class room."

Think that gets you off the hook?

Who says one has to get it in the classroom. Classroom religion is often anti-religion. Sometimes it's atheistic.

That's a religion in itself. A religion without a god. Too bad it's allowed. The god believers ought to be given equal time in the classroom... especially in the science departments.

You've gone through a good percentage of your life already. By now you ought to have learned quite a bit about the fourth "R". It's an ever-present force in our society. Something you have for yourself even if you possibly haven't joined some religious organization, such as a church. Your basic philosophy of life. What you believe the essence of life to be. What you believe about the future... after death. What you believe about the origins of the universe. And about God.

The predominate religion in America is Christianity. And though it might be difficult to know why so many denominations exist, it's good to know the basic tenets of Christianity. Either to establish your personal religious beliefs... or at least know what Christianity is all about when you begin discussing religion with someone who calls himself a Christian.

Here are the basics to Christianity:

God created man in his own image. That man (mankind) sinned against God through disobedience. But God wasn't going to leave man to self destruct. He loved his creation (especially people) too much. So after several thousand years of trying to get man straightened out, God instituted another plan. Jesus Christ was born. You know the Christmas story.

Jesus Christ wasn't only a sharp teacher, he came for a more specific purpose. He came to restore the broken relationship between man and God. This he did in a most unusual way. In some mysterious manner, he took all of man's sins, (the things that separated man from God) and bore them in himself on a cross 1900 years ago. That removed the penalty man should rightfully pay. Then, because he was superhuman (claiming to be God), he rose from the dead. What a miracle! No one else had ever done that!

Okay. As far as Christianity is concerned, all you have to do is accept what Jesus Christ has done. Believe on him and your personal sin problem is solved. Your bridge between you and God has been made.

In the process you obtain an exciting new life. New goals. New motivations. New satisfactions.

Everyone who has followed this realistic, but simple philosophy, will testify that some of the greatest benefits of Christianity are personal joy and peace. They'll be quick to invite you to try it for yourself.

That's what the fourth "R" is mainly about in America. It's not something you'll ever get graded on. Never need to graduate from it. But a lot of wise people have discovered this fourth "R" is like adding a fourth dimension to life. The dimension of depth.

Can't get that from the demanded three "R"s.

All we can say about the fourth "R" is that we've tried it . . . and it works!

WHAT TEACHERS DID YOU LIKE? WHY?

18.

FAVORITE teachers. We all have our list. Some whom we thought really knew how to teach. Those who stood out from all the rest. Some who seemed to have a special way of reaching the heart as well as the mind. True friends.

Have you ever tried to name all the teachers you have had since kindergarten days? How many have you forgotten? How many others do you wish you could forget? How many appear in your mind as an up front blur? How many do you remember more negatively than positively?

Some seemed to simply occupy space and time. You would never really call them teachers . . . only by profession.

would never really call them teachers . . . only by profession.

Probably the majority would be on your so-so list. Sure, you learned a lot from them, but you have nothing outstanding by which to identify either themselves as persons or as teachers. They seemed to enjoy what they were doing, but you thought their basic concern was to get their bi-weekly paycheck.

But in this classroom or that one you discovered a teacher whose vibes vibed with yours. You gladly list such people on your favorite teacher list.

What makes a favorite teacher a favorite?

Most likely you'd start by saying such a person really knew his subject . . . and knew how to communicate it. He kept up-to-date on the latest information available. He or she never bluffed the class. And if any unanswerable question popped up by a class member, the teacher admitted he didn't have an immediate answer. . . but promised an answer as soon as possible. That promise was always kept.

Maybe a more outstanding trait of favorite teacher: a love for students. You sensed it immediately. Even the second day in the classroom. Somehow the teacher had an uncanny ability to befriend everyone. Address students on a first name basis. Remember something about each. Be alert to their inquiries. Seem extra desirous to help each one benefit from the classroom experience. Pause to help those who found the subject appreciatively difficult . . . or to praise those who grasped it quickly. No one in the classroom was unimportant.

That's probably it. Favorite teacher lists always include teachers who made the students feel more important than the subject being taught. Teacher with a personal touch. You called them human . . . so did everyone.

Some teachers seem to teach lessons. Others teach students.

Okay, now that you've graduated, what good is a favorite teacher list except for reminiscing?

You probably list them on job applications for references. Possibly you call one or two of them now and then to seek counsel in difficult situations. You know their ears are always open to the cries of alumni. You make reference to them to support your presentations of subjects you learned from them. That's a great compliment.

But some other good things can come from making out a favorite teacher list.

Why not relist those favorite characteristics and then go to a mirror. Say to the person in the mirror, "I want to be like . . . I need some of the characteristics he possessed." Then give yourself a jab in the ribs and start a character development program.

Listing the characteristics of a favorite teacher or a favorite friend isn't a bad idea. Especially if we discover we come up short of our ideals.

Maybe we'll be teaching someone someday — either formally in a classroom or informally in an outside-of-school setting. People will be analyzing why they like us . . . or think we're passable. People do this all the time whether we're in the role of teacher, friend or fellow worker. Whether you realize it or not, someone is always sizing you up.

Getting on anyone's favorite anything list is an honor. But it demands that the listed keeps the listors confidence. Lives up to expectations.

Now that you've been graduated, you've been promoted from the student world into a world that puts a high premium on favorites.

Where has your name been listed?

DID YOU MEET THE WORLD'S GREATEST TEACHER?

19.

WORLD'S GREATEST? If you sat in the same classrooms I've endured, you'd probably be able to compile a list of the world's worst. Or else an unending list of the world's mediocre.

Of course, most of us have trouble due to our limited perspectives. We're standing too close to put "greatest" in front of any teacher's name. We need to make an appraisal of historical personages. Usually it's only as someone becomes a part of history that he becomes known for his greatness.

So let's go back a few years.

The time: 450-400 B.C. Place: Athens. A continual

talker roams the streets of the city. Attracts crowds in the marketplace or his favorite spots—the gymnasia. He's particularly capable of spotting youths with keen minds who sought a reason for being. Was primarily concerned with abstract ideas, especially the concepts of the psyche — soul, and concepts of right and wrong.

Best known for his admonition, "Know thyself."

Believed the psyche as the life force of every person. Sought out those who'd argue intelligently. Searched for definitions of the abstract. Concentrated on the intellectual consciousness of man.

But he never wrote anything. Yet Socrates has been given credit for laying the philosophical foundations of Western culture. Information about his personality and doctrine are found chiefly in the dialogues of Plato. Socrates, the first of a trio of great philosophers. Plato and Aristotle the other two.

Because Socrates was a mile out front of the thinking and thinkers of his day, he was misunderstood and constantly accused — usually of corrupting the minds of youth. In 399 B.C. he was indicted for "impiety," "corrupting the minds of the young" and "neglect of the god whom the city worshiped." Found guilty. Sentenced to death. Died after given a cup of hemlock in prison.

Considered throughout the ages as one of the world's greatest teachers.

Now let's knock at the door of the 20th Century. In Ulm, Germany, a baby boy entered the world on March 14, 1879. He'd grow not only to become an accomplished violinist, but with a mind and heart that soar into the cosmos. Considered later as one of the most creative intellects of human history.

In 1933, when Adolph Hitler became chancellor of Germany, Albert Einstein renounced his German citizenship. Came to Princeton University. Germany's loss, America's gain!

Lived a simple life. Devoted himself to continual study of advanced science... especially physics. But he also delved deep into the philosophy of pacifism. Spent almost as much time espousing pacifism as discussing science. But his formula $E=mc^2$ (Energy = mass x velocity of light) opened the door to the nuclear age.

In between these two great men lived another Teacher.

Western world revolved around him. Dates on calendars begin with the year of his birth. Taught only three years, but his teachings have altered history. Basic teaching centers in love — by God, toward God, because of God... to men regardless of national origin, race, intellectual capacity.

More written about him than any other person in history. More people in America identify with him than with any other person living or dead.

His greatest teachings not in abstract philosophy or scientific theory. His teachings have a life changing dynamic.

He proclaimed, "I came that you might have life and have it more abundantly." Those who delve into his teaching discover this to be true.

He boldly proclaimed, "I am the way, the truth and

the life." The way to God. The only way to eternity.

One writer, who had experienced a dramatic conversion to this greatest Teacher, put it rather clearly: "If any one be in Christ, he is a new creature. Old things pass away; behold, all things become new."

In contrast to Socrates, Einstein or the others whom you might be able to list among the world's greats, you can meet Jesus Christ on a personal basis. There's proof that he participated in a miracle no one else could do. He rose from the dead. Read the reports of Matthew, Mark, Luke and John in the New Testament. All of them confirm his aliveness. And from there, go on to investigate his life changing teachings. Allow his love to penetrate your psyche . . . and your relationships with others.

Your life will never be the same. It'll become new . . . exciting . . . worthwhile.

An encounter with Jesus Christ — the World's Greatest Teacher — starts with faith . . . yours! Get a Bible. Take his teachings at face value. You'll discover the richest, deepest, most rewarding meanings life has to offer.

No one else has ever guaranteed his teachings to perform in this manner. Discover his truth . . . but be careful. Jesus Christ will change your life!

THE SCHOOL FROM WHICH YOU'LL NEVER GRADUATE

20.

GO TO SCHOOL forever? Incredible! Haven't we been talking about the joys and responsibilities of being graduated? Haven't we looked at graduation as the termination of schooling?

You ain't never going to get us back into school, some avow.

Not in some formal classroom setting. Not in the regimentation of the past.

You've graduated from all that.

Yet there's a school from which you'll never graduate. One which produces continual lessons. Which draws upon your accumulated knowledge and know-how.

Which demands even more than most teachers or professors.

It's the school into which you have graduated, not from which you have graduated. No alma mater here. No diploma.

In this new school, you're expected to learn just like in the good old days. With a few exceptions. No putting off learning or studying of the answers until some final exam hour. You are expected to learn on the spot. Sometimes the teacher won't even repeat the instructions. Sometimes you'll have to figure out the answers without any teacher present. And you can't afford to fail. Failures are often eliminated. Someone else is capable of taking your place.

Call it the school of experience. The school of hard knocks. The world of work. Life.

You're in it for life!

You can take two approaches to your new schooling. In it for life . . . like a lifetime prison sentence. In it for life . . . as a lifelong challenge. One considering it a drudgery, fatalistically hoping that the end will come. The other considering it as a challenge.

To ever apply what you have learned. To develop creative ways to use your accumulated knowledge or partially developed skills. To produce in such a manner that reflects the fact you have been well educated.

The school of experience can either be a cruel taskmaster or an excitement producing, probing force that challenges the best in you to surface. Like cream in fresh dairy milk.

No set pattern for lesson learning. Some lessons

come in clusters... some singly. Sometimes you'll have long periods of dull non-learning, even drudgery. On the other hand, you might be bombarded.

Can't say, "I'll learn a little every day... just like in the classroom." Today's teacher isn't that organized... or that patient. Learn it now. Fast.

No shutting off learning encounters. No matter how old you become... or if you reach retirement age. You'll still be faced with new data, new approaches. Learn or lag behind. No other choice in our fast paced world.

Ah! That's the joy of living. Facing continual changes and challenges. Developing new concepts. Applying new techniques.

Life is exciting. A never-ending learning continuum. Join the crowd.

But there's something better than a diploma awaiting you. Along the way you'll make others happy... and even become happy. Happy to accomplish something new. Something beneficial to others.

And if you've had an encounter with the World's Greatest Teacher about which we spoke in Chapter 19, when you approach the end of life, having done your best, you'll probably hear his words, "Well done, good and faithful servant, enter into the joy of your reward." That would be the greatest graduation ever.

In the meantime, while attending the school of experience, do everything to be worthy of the diploma awaiting you then!